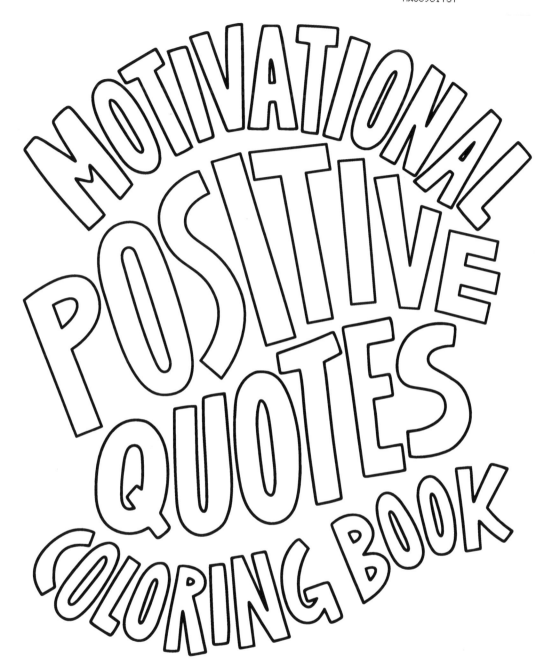

This book belongs to:

_____

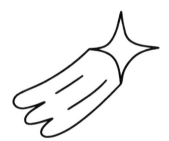

HAPPINESS IS A JOURNEY NOT A DESTINATION

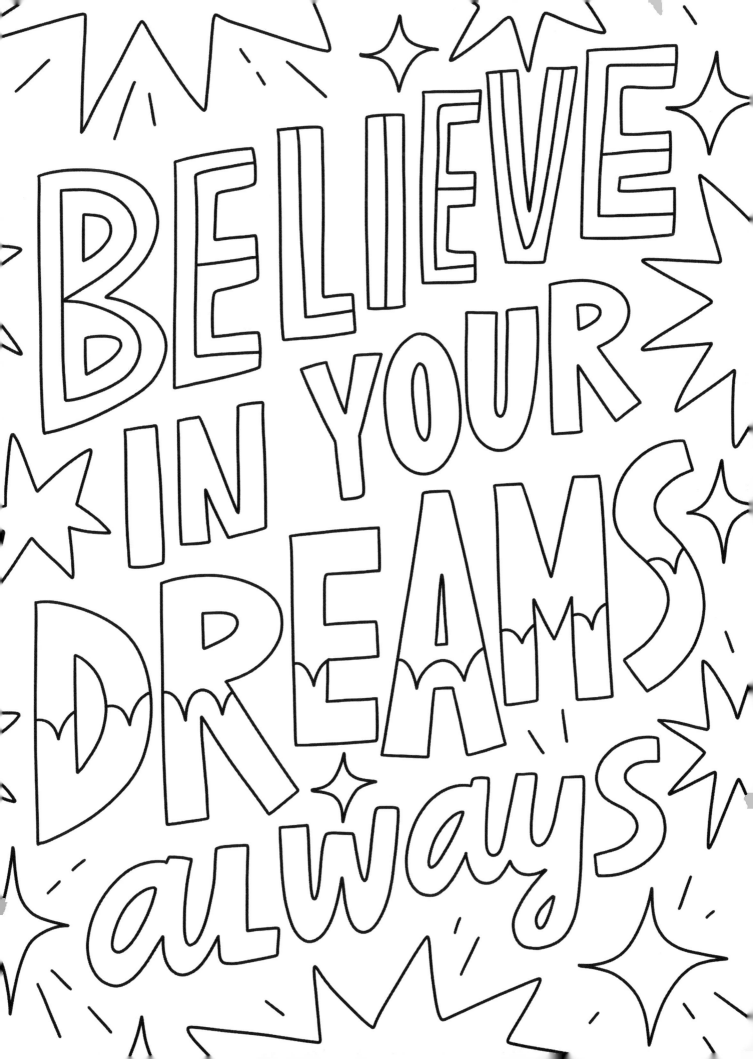

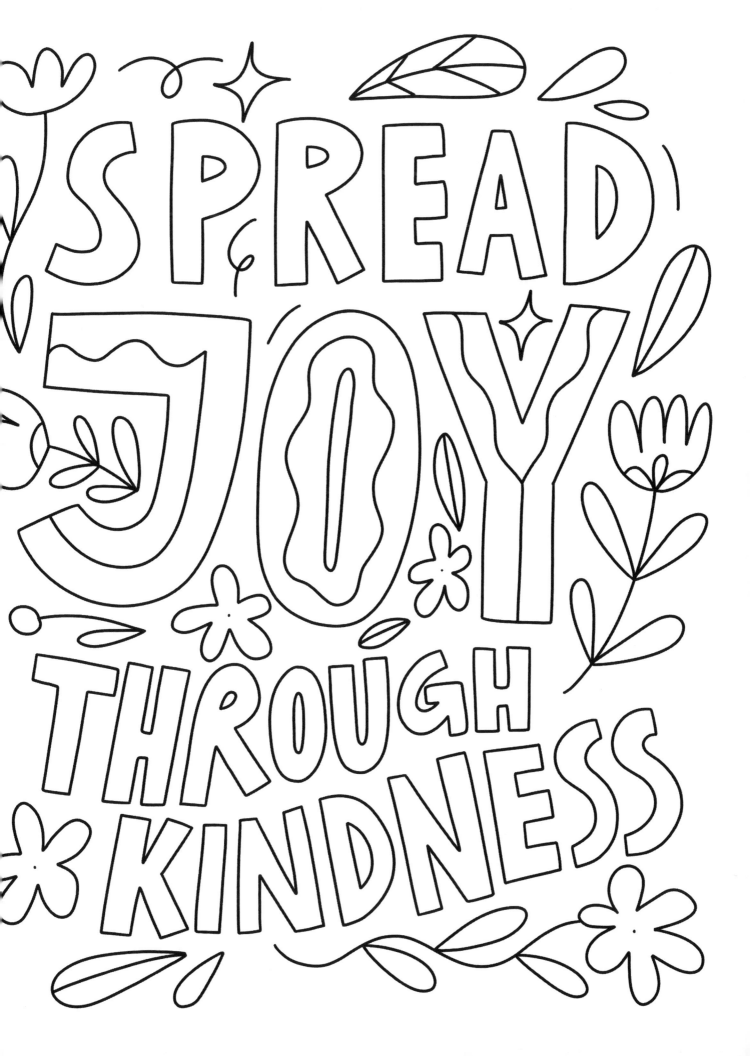

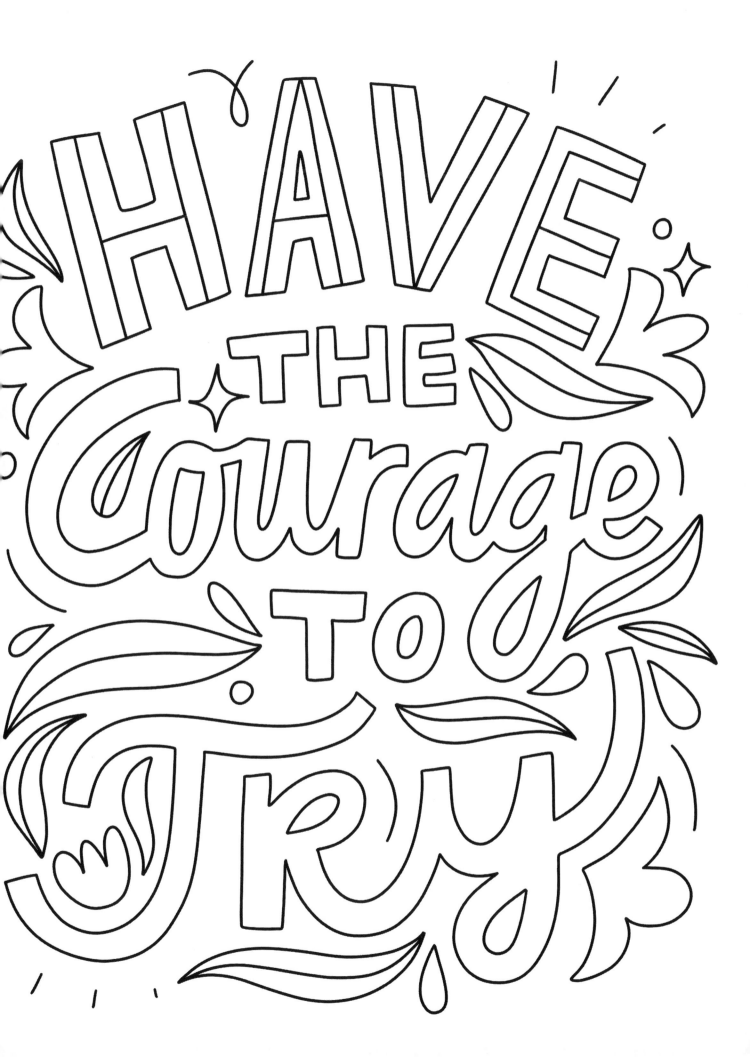

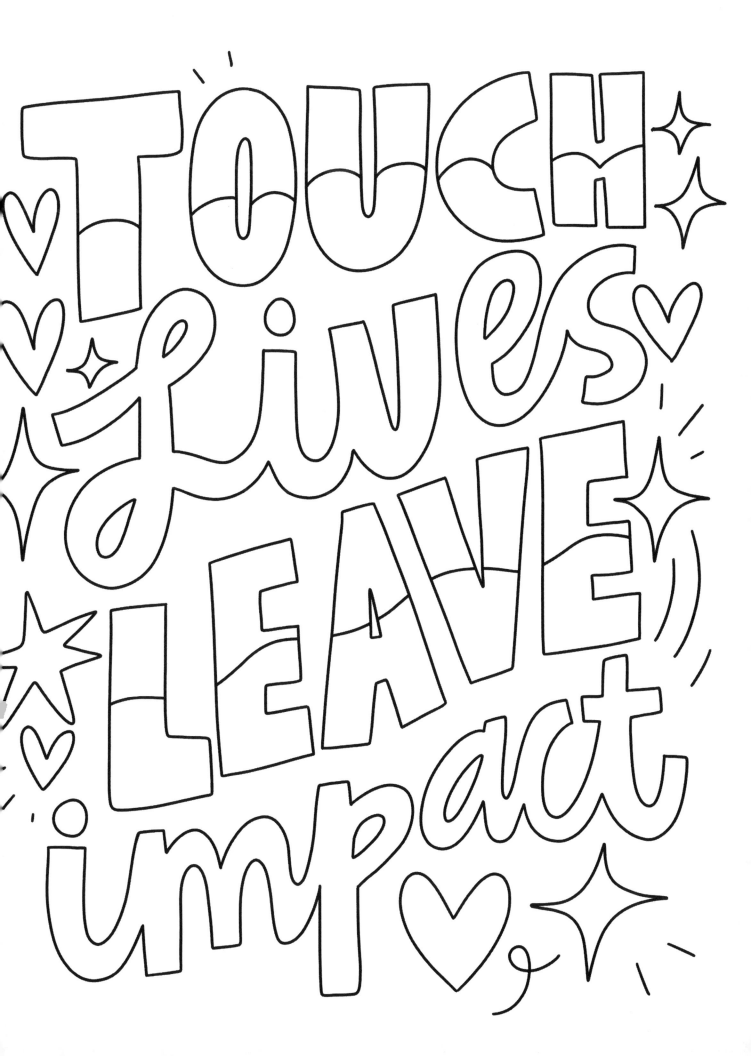

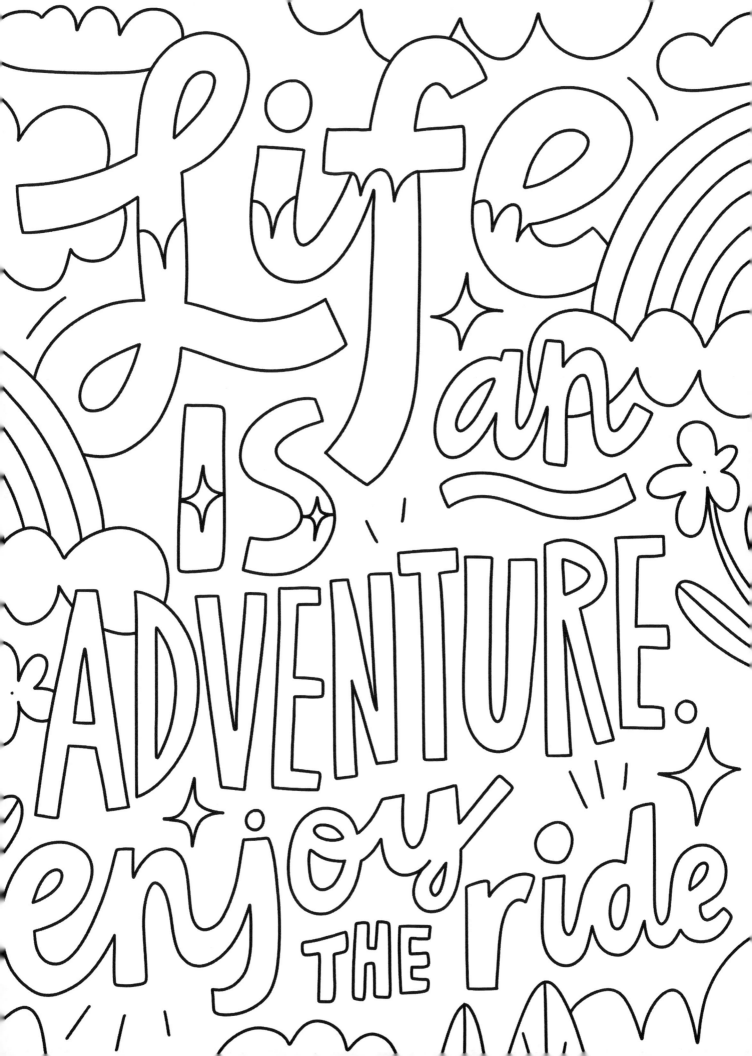

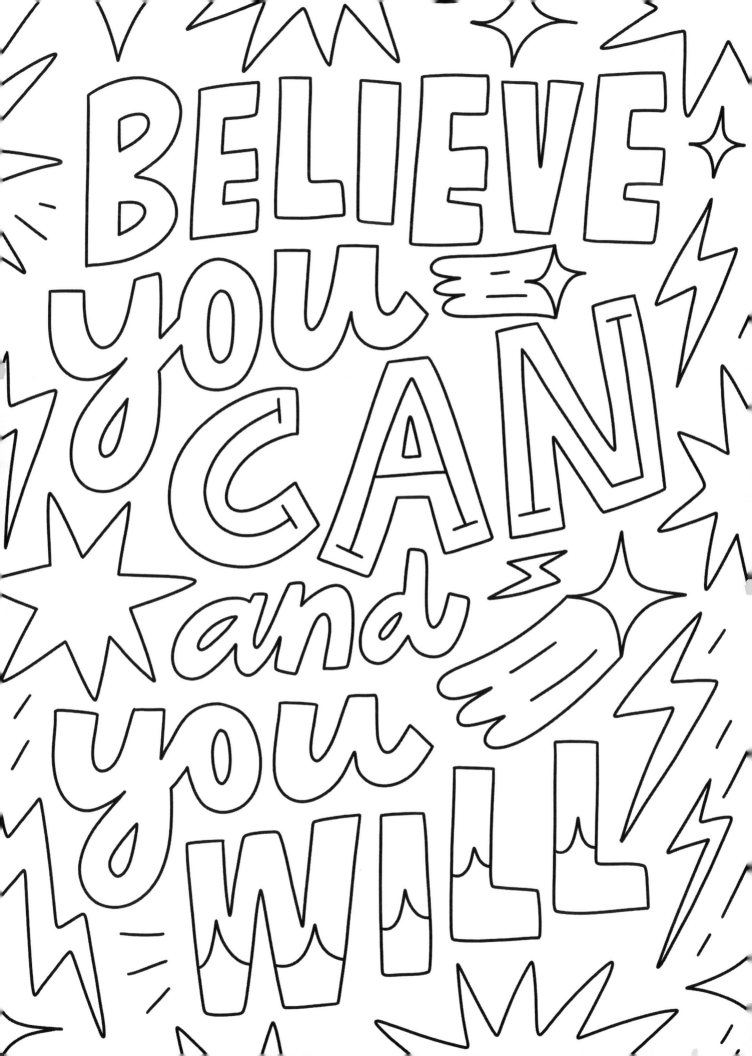

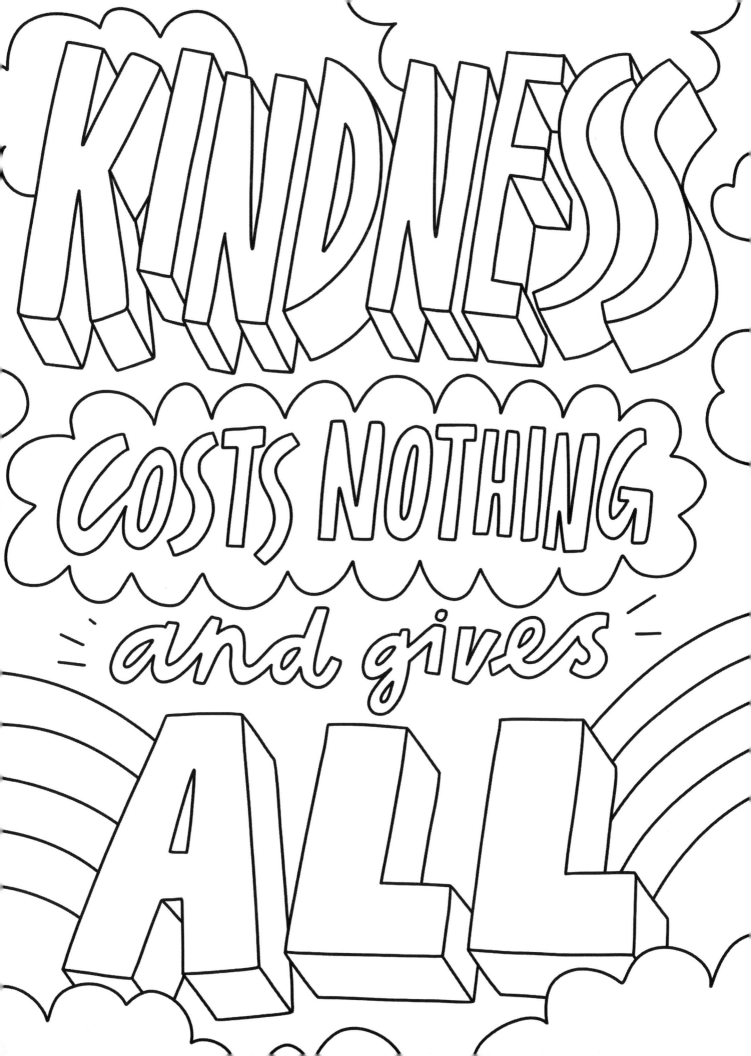

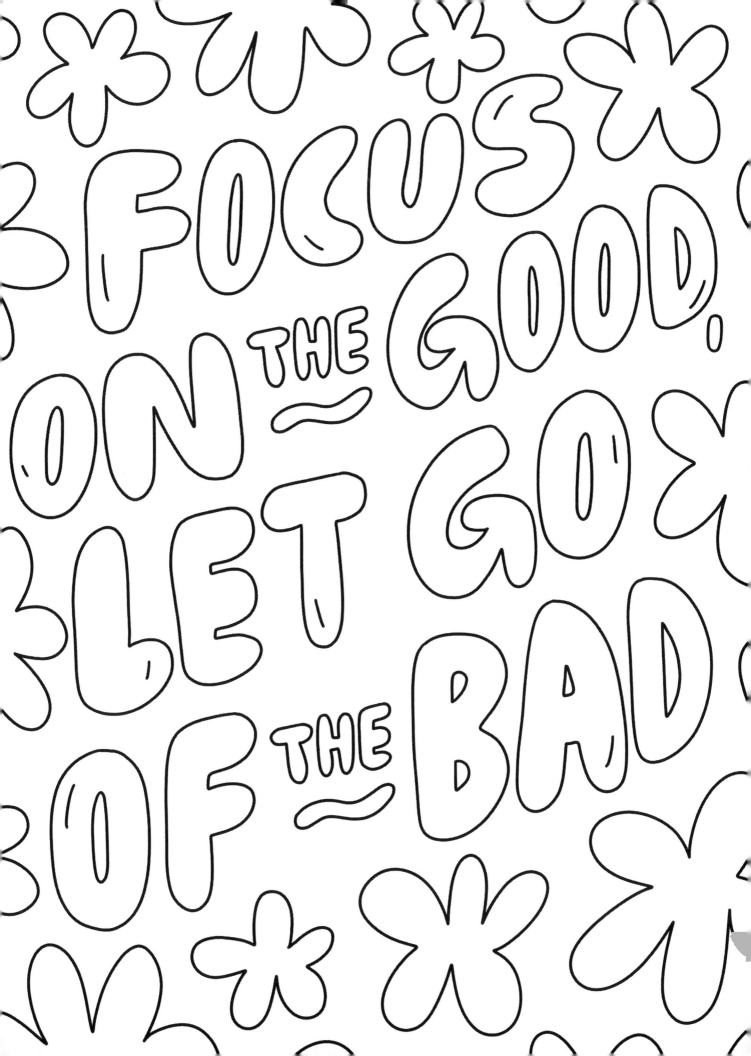

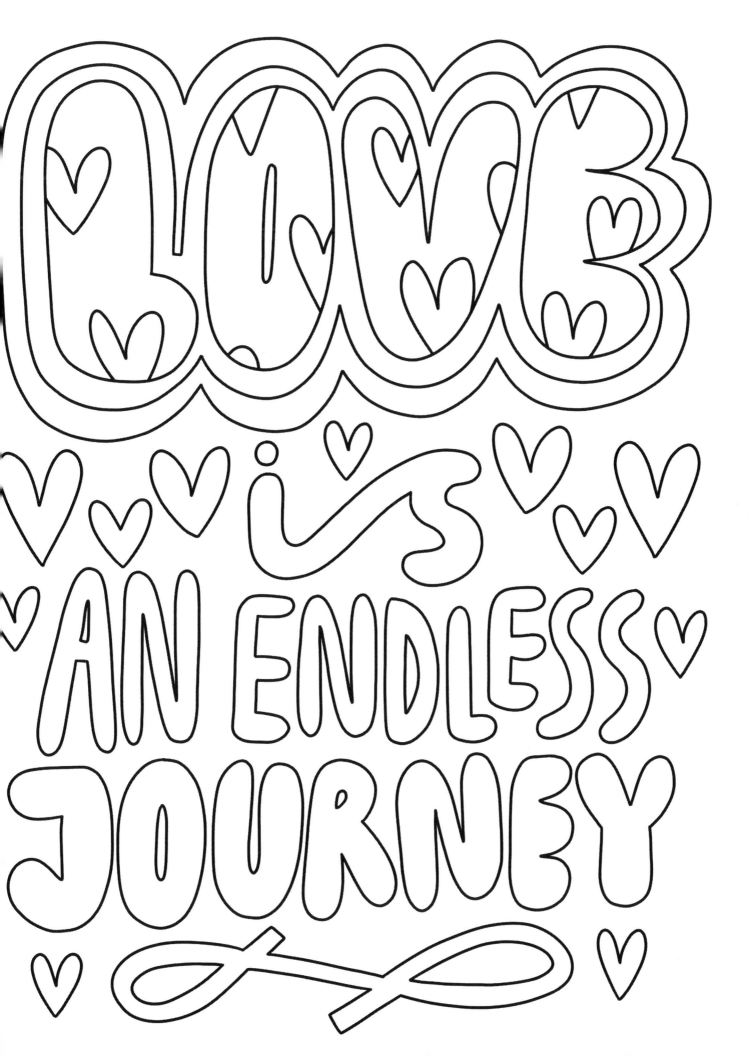

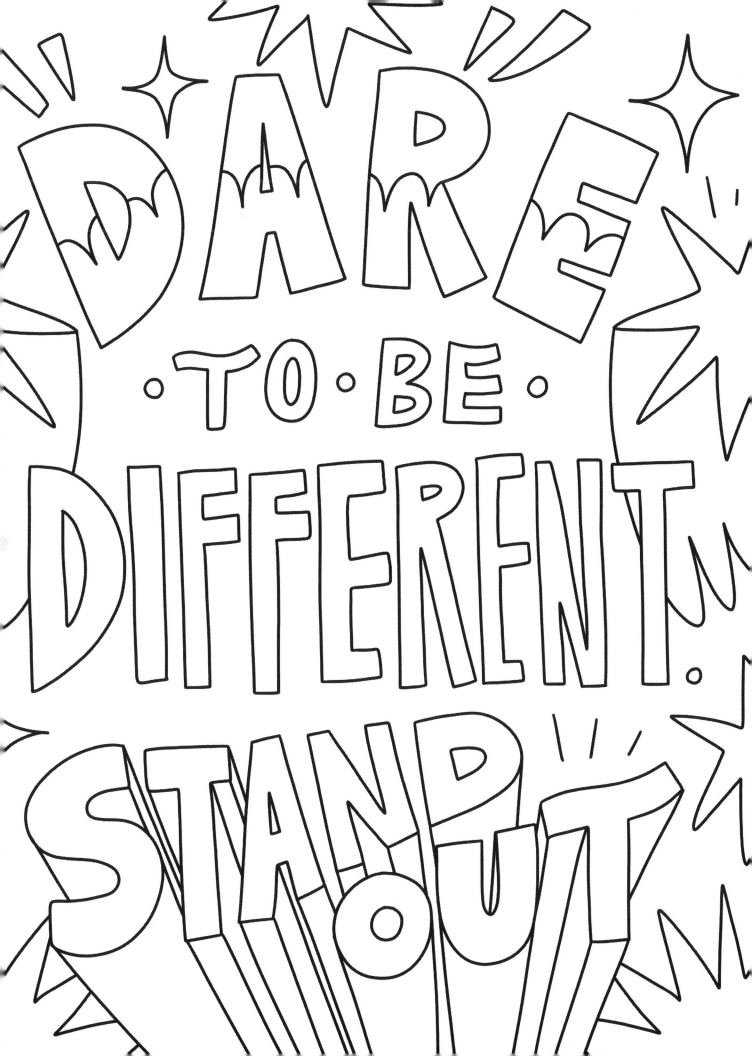

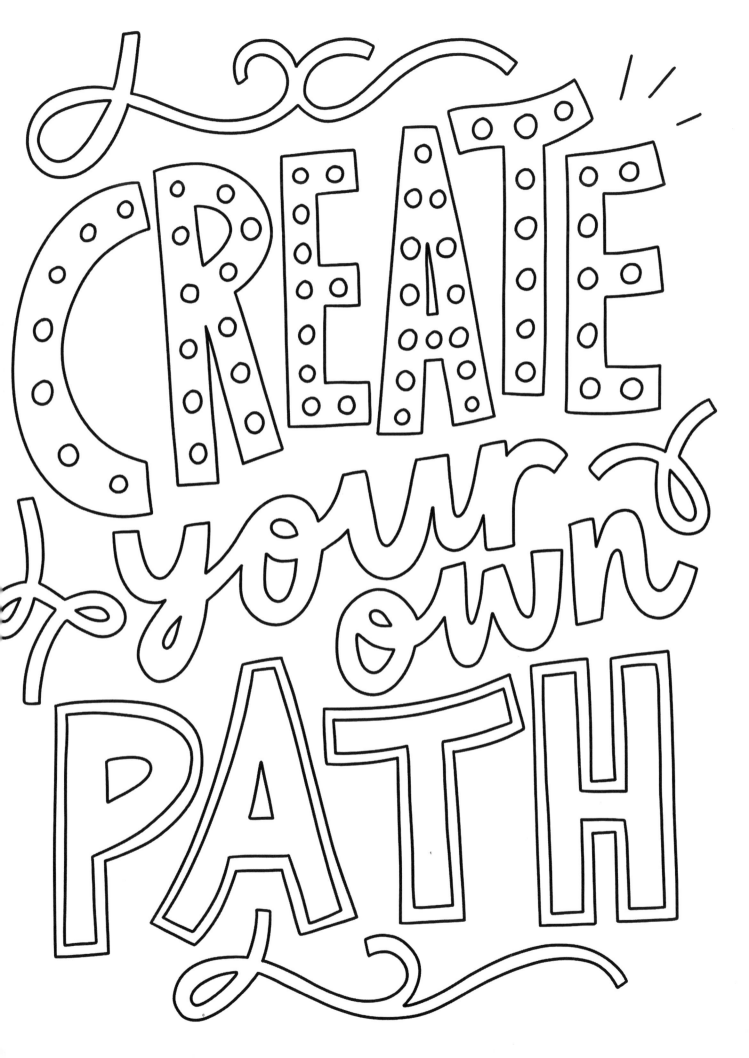

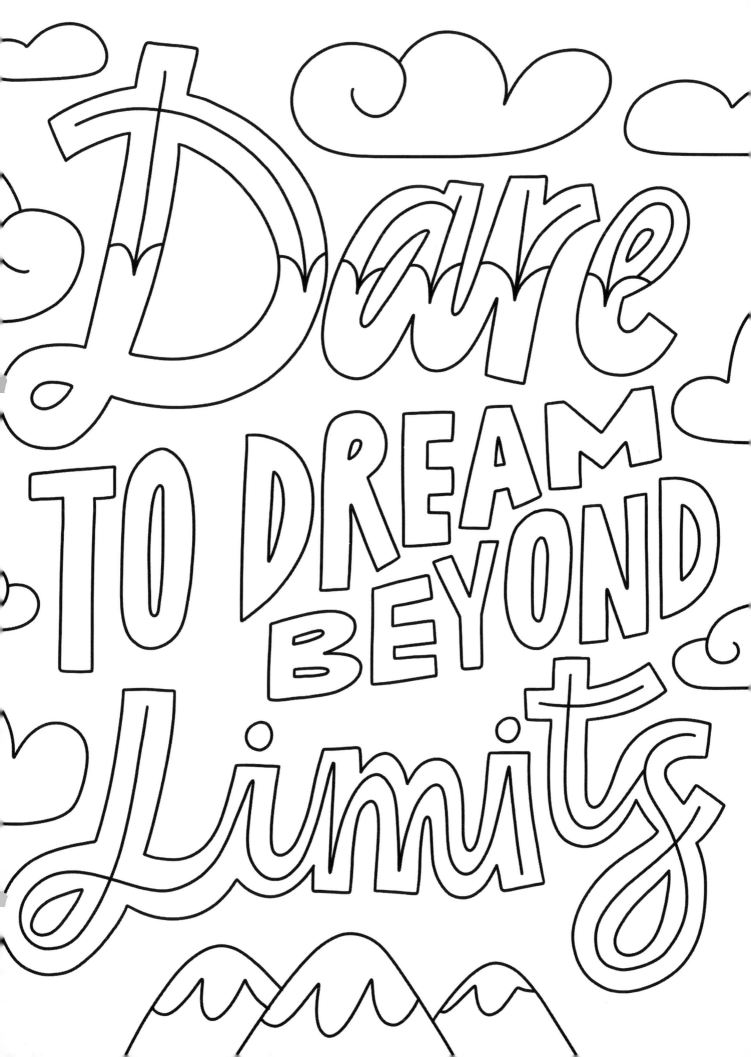

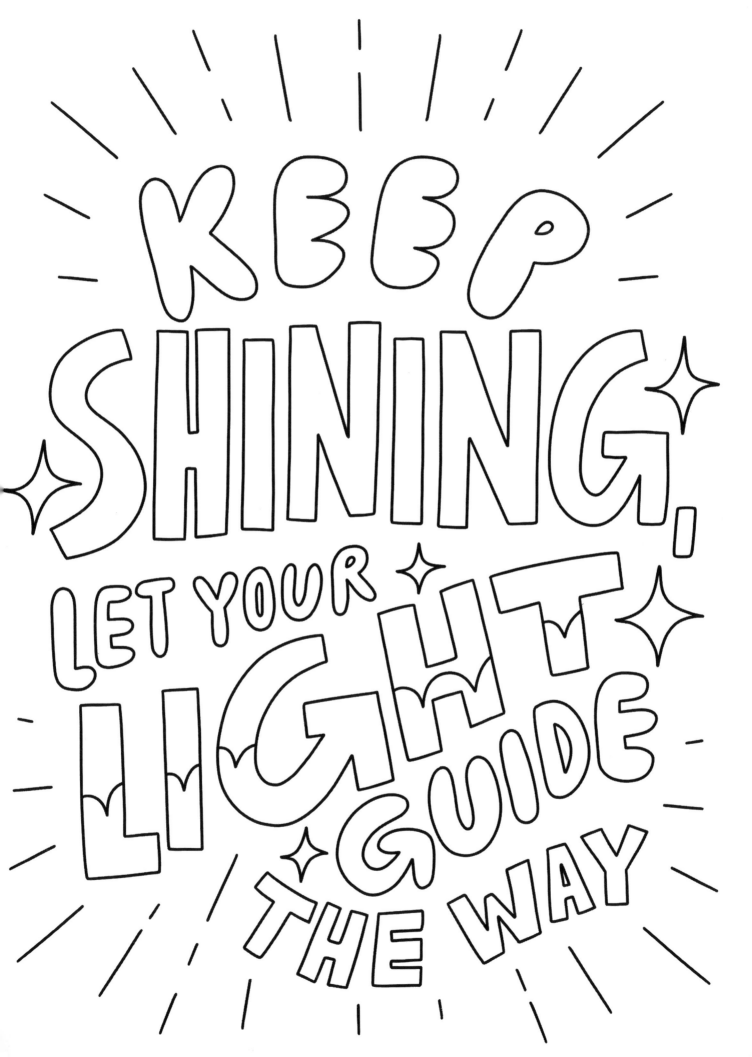

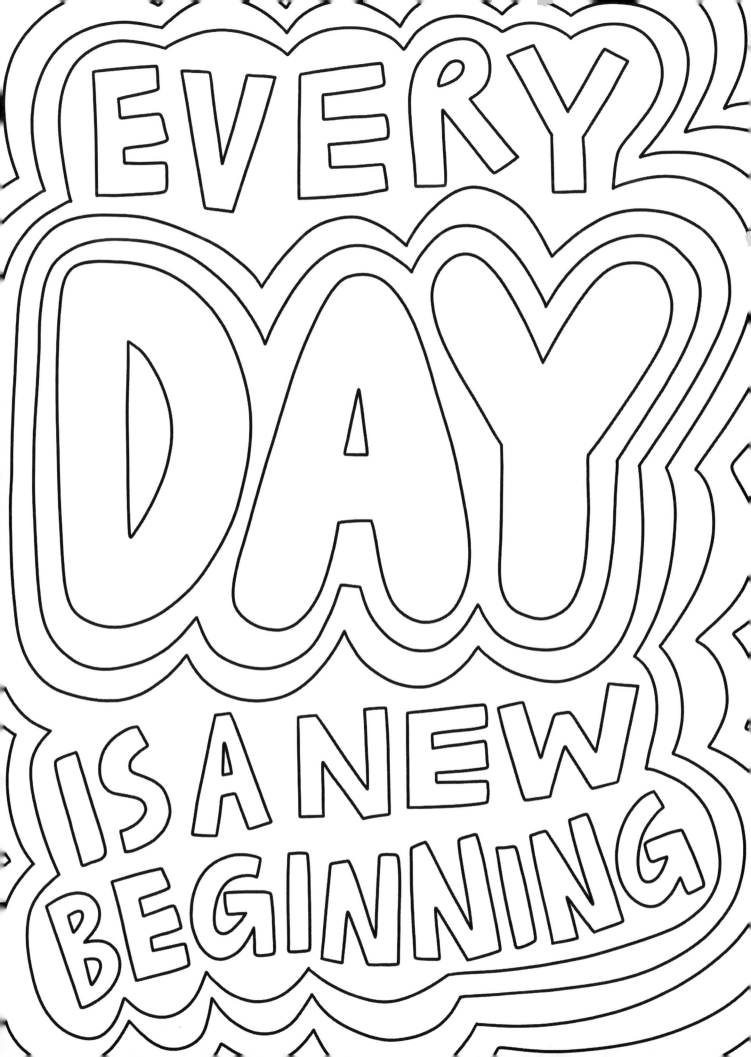

the only LIMIT is the one you set for yourself

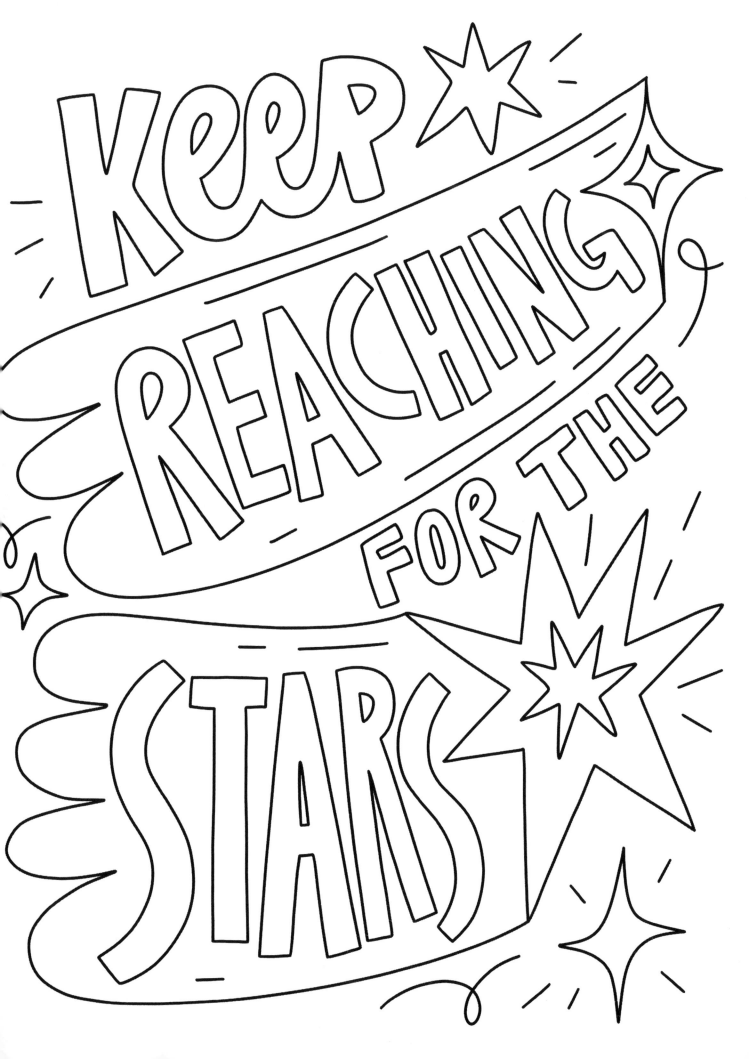

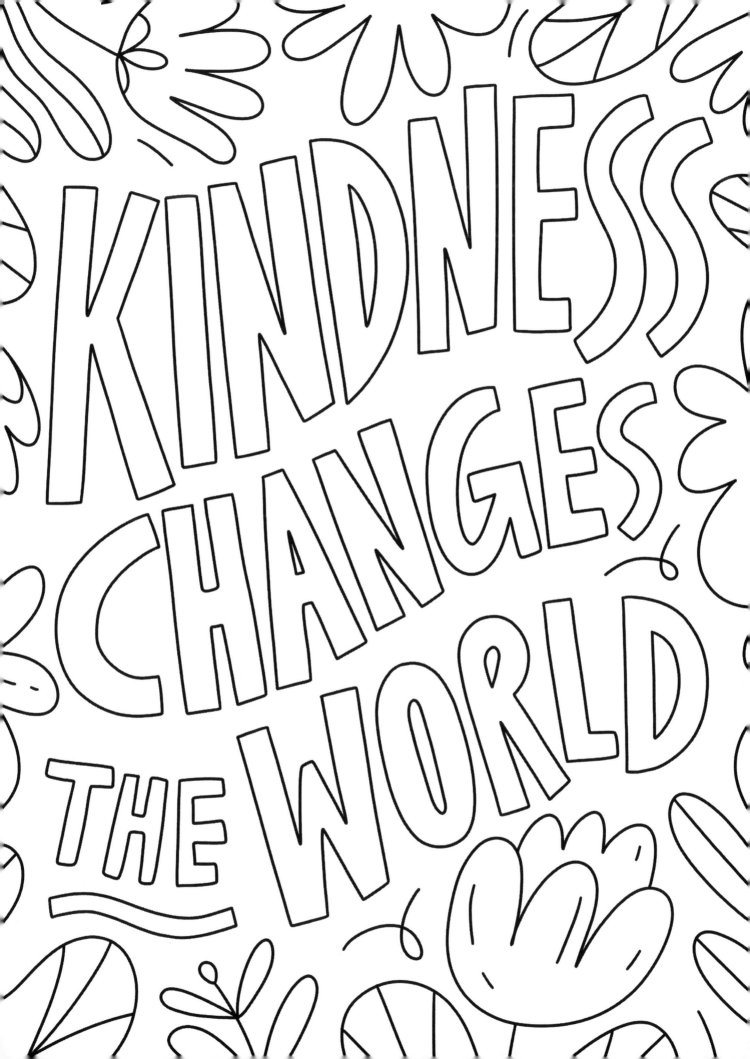

Don't wait for opportunities create them yourself

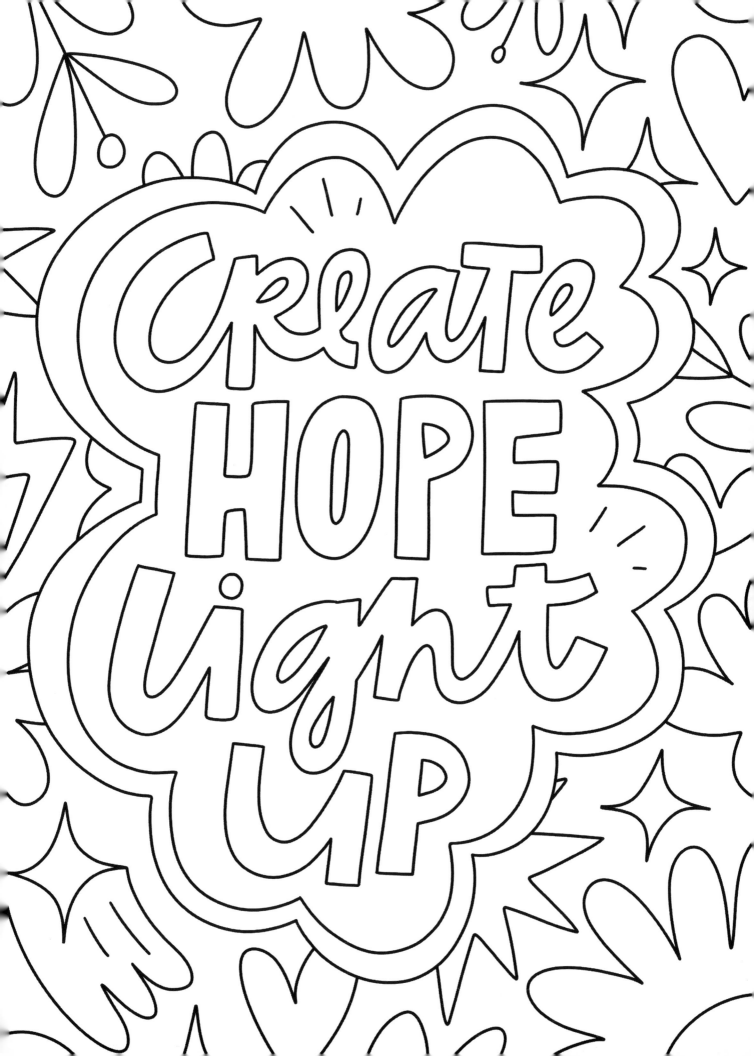

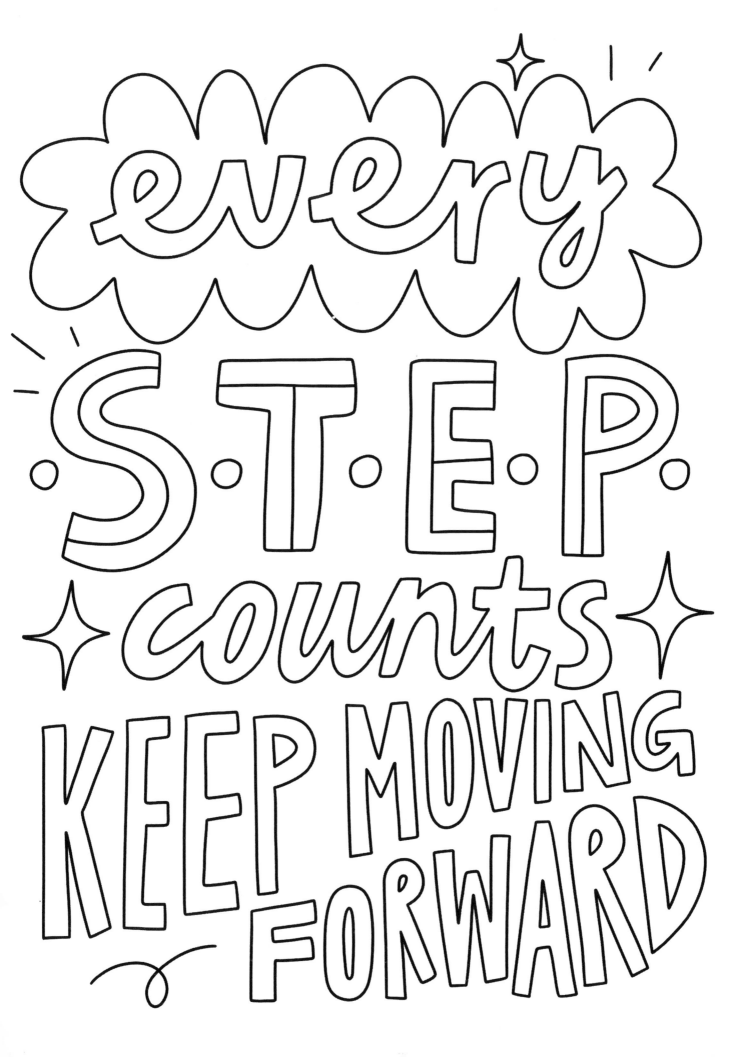

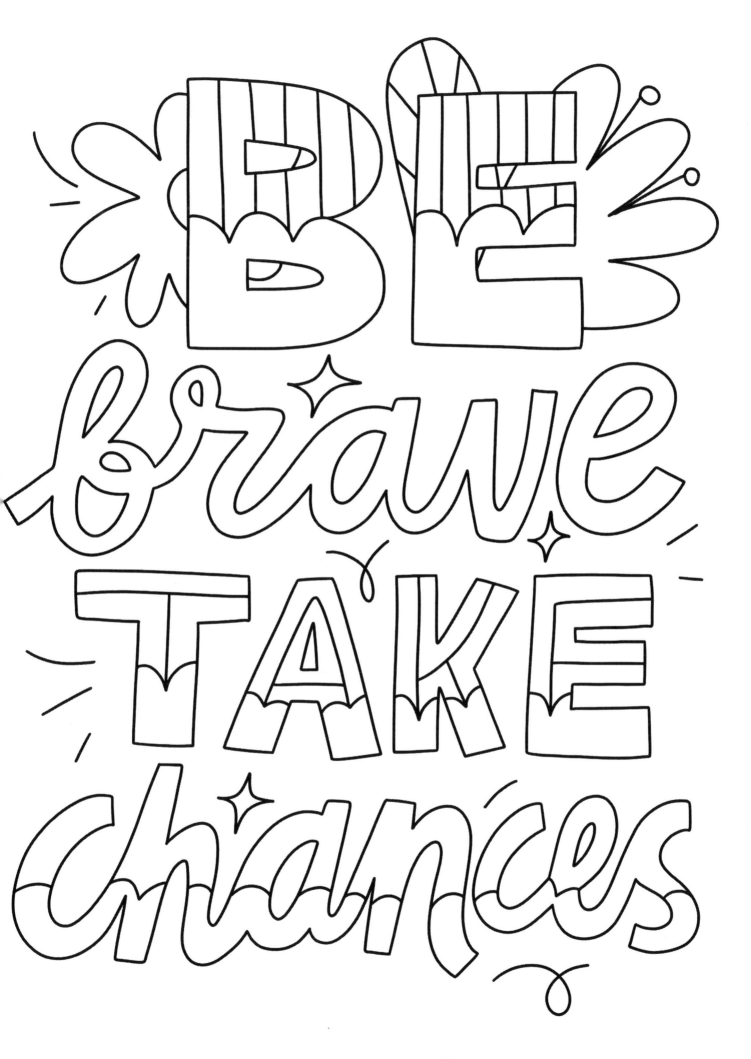

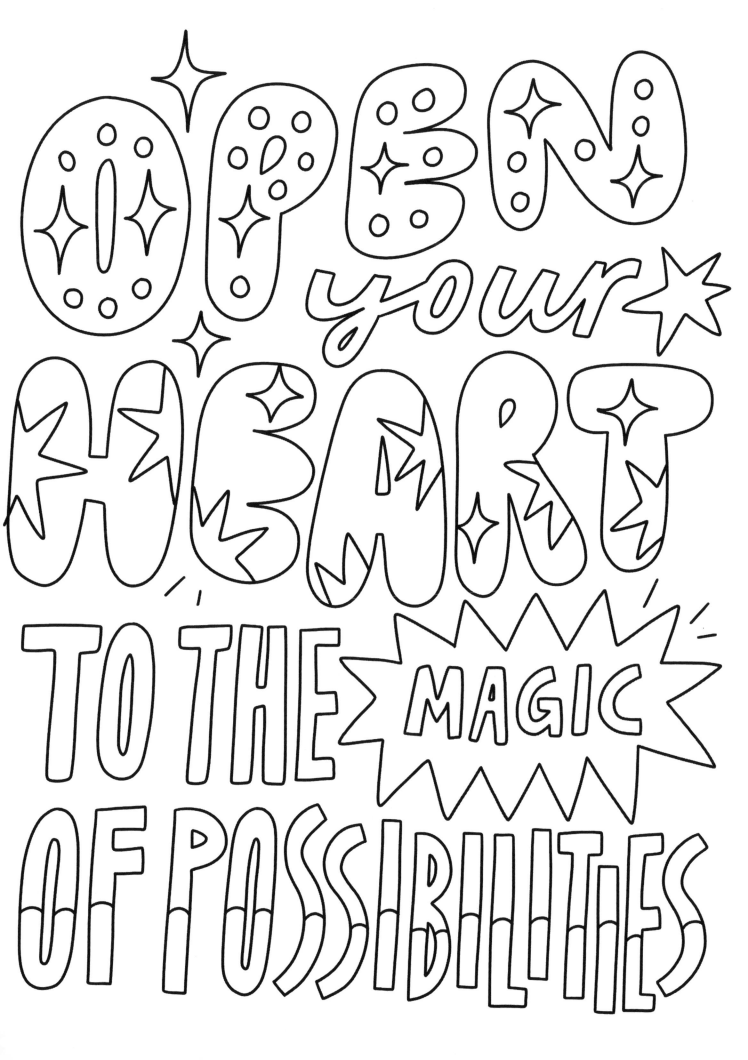

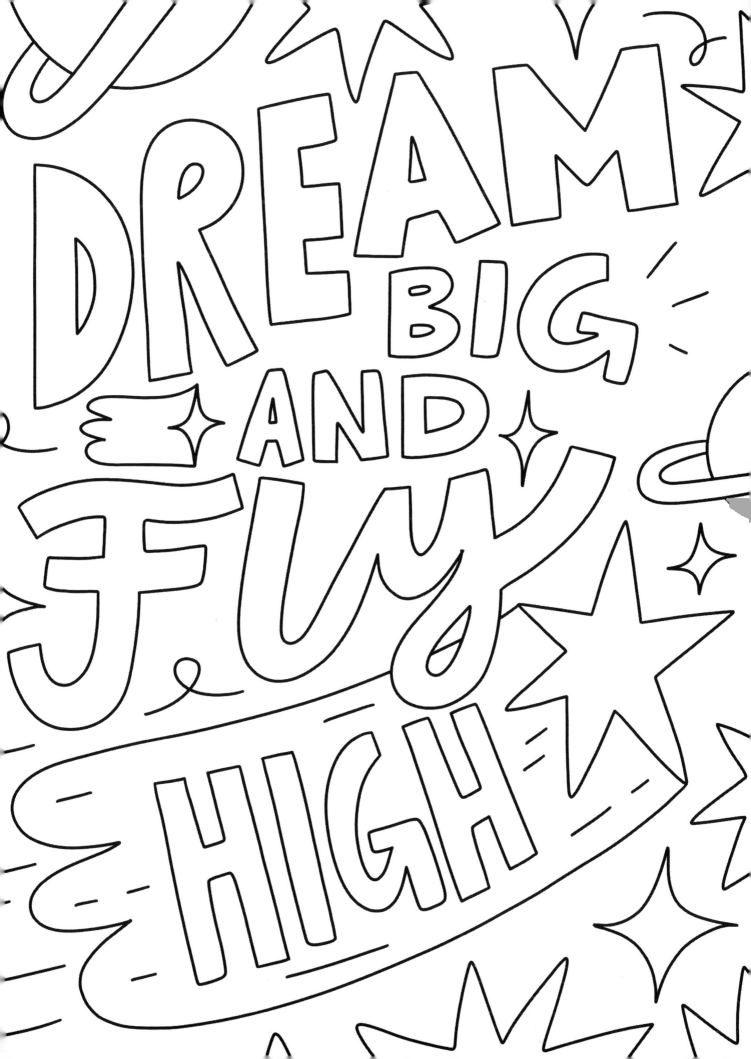

Made in the USA
Las Vegas, NV
04 October 2024